Cooking for FREEALITEA

Wellness Teas, Tonics, and Tails for a stress-FREE Reality

By Dr. Michelle Clay, DO, CHHC

COPYRIGHT PAGE

Copyright © 2022 by FREEALITEA

Published by freealitea.com

FREEALITEA 2480 Briarcliff Rd Ste 6 #194 Atlanta, GA 30329

www.freealitea.com

This book contains material protected under international and federal copyright laws and treaties. Any unauthorized reprint or use of this material is prohibited. No part of this book may be reproduced or transmitted in any form or by any means, electronic or mechanical, including photocopying, recording, or by any information storage and retrieval system without express written permission from the publisher except in the case of brief quotations embodied in critical articles and reviews.

Limit of Liability / Disclaimer of Warranty: While the publisher and author have used their best efforts in preparing this book, they make no representations or warranties with the respect to the accuracy or completeness of the contents of this book and specifically disclaim any implied warranties of fitness for a particular purpose. No warranty may be created or extended by sales representatives or written sales materials.

The advice and strategies contained herein may not be suitable for your situation.

You should consult with a doctor where appropriate. Neither the publisher nor author shall be liable for any loss or damages including but not limited to special, incidental, consequential or other damages.

FREEALITEA books and products are available through online book retailers. To contact Freealitea.com directly, call our Customer Service Department within the U.S. at 504-345-8671

Table of Contents

Introduction 1

CHAPTER 2 TONICS 5
    Digestive Relief Tonic 9
    Cleanse & Calm Tonic 11
    Cleanse & Calm Cocktail 12
    Cleanse & Calm Simple Syrup 13
    Mindset & Mood Tonic 19
    Mindset & Mood Foot Tonic 21
    Mindset & Mood Aromatherapy 23

CHAPTER 3 SMOOTHIES 25
    Royal Berry Blast 29
    Release & Relieve Turmeric Smoothie 31
    Purify Green Dream Juice 37
    Purify & Pineapple Smoothie 39
    Stress FREELIFE Smoothie 41
    Berry Blast Stress-FREE Smoothie 43
    Chocolate Smoothie 45
    Citrus Rise & Shine 47
    Release, Rise & Island Shine Smoothie 49
    Chill & Chai Warm Smoothie 51

CHAPTER 4 TAILS – Mocktails or the G & G version 53
    Release Your ImmuniTEA Tail 55
    Immune Berry Spritzer 57
    Berries & Bubbles 59
    Release Romance ChocolaTEAni 61
    Royale RoyalTEA 63
    RoyalTEANI 65

Royal Carnival 67
R&R Sangria 69
Rise & Shine Sangria 71
Rise & Shine Toddy 73
Release Relieve & Sparkle 75
RootTEAni 79
Pink Ginger Sunrise 81
Fancy FREETEAni 83

CHAPTER 5 SOUPS & SALADS 85

Fall Harvest Salad 87
Purification Breakfast 89
Full Spectrum Stress Release Salad with Release Recharge Vinaigrette 91
FREEALITAL Stew 93
Release & Purify Green Soup 97
Relieve Sweet Potato Soup 101
Golden Broccoli Soup 105
Rise Caribbean Black Bean Soup 109

CHAPTER 6 SWEETS 111

Romance ChocolaTEA Truffles 115
Raw Berry Crisp with Cashew Cream and Release Your ImmuniTEA Glaze 117
Sweet & Nice & Everything Chai (Sweet Potato Chai Muffins) 121
Comfy-Cozy Apple Cinnamon Cookies 125

CHAPTER 7 LAGNIAPPE 127

Creole Jambalaya with a FREEALITEA Spin 131
FREEALITEA's Gumbo Z'herbes 135
Citrus Dressing Marinade 139
Apple Cider Reduction Vinaigrette 141
Release Recharge Simple Syrup 143
Release Your ImmuniTEA Simple Syrup 145
Release Recharge Cherry Vinaigrette 147

Introduction

The world has had a love affair with tea for many years. Tea derives from the plants in the Camellia family originating in central China and Japan. As lore and legend go, Shennong which translates to "Divine Farmer", is credited with "discovering" tea. As the story goes, Shennong was taking a rest from his labor under a tree, a Camellia tree and decided to boil some water to refresh himself. Dried leaves fell from its branches landed in his pot as it was boiling and infused to make a new drink to his palate. Voila! The beginning of tea. Per the purists "true tea" is ONLY from the Camellia plant. Per that definition, there are four types of tea:

1) Black

2) Green

3) White

4) Oolong.

It is important to note, that the creation of tea with leaves from a Camellia plant were an infusion. An infusion is simply a part of a plant whether that is leaf, flower, or root, combined with water and allowed to boil or steep to extract its flavor and essence. With this in mind, technically any infusion with part of a plant could be considered a tea.

Rooibos tea also known as Bush Tea is native to South Africa. The San, also known as the Bushmen, were the aboriginal people of South Africa. They were a hunting and gathering group that lived on the land 100,000 years BEFORE other Black and European settlers. The Bushmen used the leaves of the Aspalathus Linearis plant, rooibos, for a drink and as an herbal remedy for different ailments.

I too have a love affair with tea. It has changed my life in beautiful ways. At one point I felt like it saved my life, both physically and emotionally.

My love affair with tea actually began out of necessity. Like most, my upbringing involved iced tea, the Lipton kind. When I was young, both of my grandmothers were involved in the Missionary Society, Church Women United, craft clubs, and other organizations. When they would have the "ladies" over for a "meeting", I was charged with helping to set the table. That's when the fancy silverware in the velvet lined box and other special occasion dishes and serving utensils would come out. The beverage of choice was iced tea. It would be served from a fancy glass pitcher with a serving container of sugar. Sometimes fresh mint leaves were added. I remember no matter how much sugar I added, it never quite tickled my fancy because all of the sugar would just swirl at the bottom never mixing in right. I would try to drink some so that I could feel like a society lady too. From my young perspective, iced tea was a "grown up" thing that didn't quite tickle my fancy. I would stick with my Kool-Aid and Hawaiian Punch.

But tea took on a new meaning in 2007. 2007 was a pivotal year for me. On January 1, 2007, I said to myself, "Be very clear on what it is you are doing. Anything you initiate this year, will be multiplied to the nth degree in the future." 2007 was my special birthday year, 07/07/07. I thought with triple 7s, there must be magic awaiting me!

In September of 2007, as I was walking through the San Juan, Puerto Rico airport, my body gave out. With each step, my legs felt heavier and heavier and breathing became more difficult. The world went black for a second and I passed out. Right in front of the gate where my flight was departing. I was embarrassed because I was a flight attendant at the time and here I am sprawled on the floor uniform and everything! The paramedics were called but I refused to go to the hospital in Puerto Rico, so I was allowed to fly home and follow up with my doctor the next day. At my doctor's visit, the Physician did a rapid test of my blood to check my hemoglobin. The machine read "LO", no numbers came up, just "LO". From there, everything went into a frenzy. She said, "I'm calling an ambulance right now to take you to the hospital. This means your hemoglobin is below 5.0 and you need a transfusion immediately!"

Me being the strong-minded woman I am, I refused ambulance transport and stated I would drive myself to the hospital. My doctor refused and said she would not permit me to drive because I could pass out on the way there even though the hospital was only 7 minutes away. We came to an agreement that I would take a cab. Once I arrived in the ER, testing showed that my hemoglobin was 3.3. Please note that normal is between 12.0 – 16.0. Most menstruating women may fall around 10.0 – 11.0, especially if you are a vegetarian as I am.

The ER Physician wanted to transfuse 3 units of blood stat! She said with a hemoglobin that low, I could have a heart attack or stroke at any time and die! I refused the transfusion. When I refused, they even called my mother! Here I am 36 years old, and they called my mother to "tell on me" like I was sent to the principal's office! Her reply, "She is grown and can make her own decisions. I know my daughter and trust her decision."

I called my spiritual mother Yemi Jones who was a Master Herbalist and natural healing helper. She and her husband Hank Jones were an elder couple who had a wellness center in Cottonwood, Alabama called The Purification Garden. When I tell you, the miracles in wellness and I healing I witnessed there would blow your mind! Anyhoo, Miss Yemi said, "I can't tell you what to do, but if you decide not to get the transfusion, I have something that can help you."

After 12 hours in the ER, I signed out AMA (against medical advice) and took a cab back to my car so I could drive myself home. That night was scary! My heart was beating so fast, and I couldn't get it to slow down. I kept hearing the words in my head, "You could have a heart attack or stroke at any time." I prayed and asked for more time. I wasn't ready to go yet. There was still so much for me to do in this life! God saw fit to allow me to make it through the night. The next day, I got on a train from Philadelphia where I was living to Washington D.C. to Hank and Yemi Jones of the Purification Garden. Thankfully for me, they were visiting in D.C. for a few months so I could get to them easily. When I arrived, Miss Yemi gave me some type of tea I had never seen before. It was a dark green color and kind of grainy with a mild flavor. I drank that tea three times per day for three days. It was nice and smooth especially when adding a little fresh lime juice and tupelo honey. My head began to feel a little clearer and my body a little stronger. Sometimes you don't know how sick you are until you start to feel better. It's like the fog slowly dissipating as the sun peaks through the clouds.

Two weeks later, I had my follow up appointment with my PCP. When she checked my hemoglobin, it was 6.7. All I had was Miss Yemi's tea which she named Miss Yemi's Green Purification Tea. No iron pills, nothing! Just Miss Yemi's tea and A LOT of green vegetables, beets, and turnips.

***Disclaimer, I'm not suggesting you refuse your Physician's recommendation for a blood transfusion or other medical interventions if you are experiencing anemia.

That experience forever changed my perspective AND RESPECT for tea, herbs, and plant technology.

Miss Yemi taught me so much about herbs and the power of plant medicine. I went to her every time I had a minor health challenge or just wanted a tune up to maintain my wellness goals. And trust me, Miss Yemi's Green Purification Tea was a staple of my wellness plan. But when Miss Yemi passed away, she took the formula of the Purification Tea with her. When she went on to Glory, I felt lost and floating in the wind. Not only was she a teacher and a mentor, but she was also a mother to me. She stepped in right on time when I was flailing along after my mother passed away from breast cancer in 2007. Though she didn't birth me from her womb, I loved her like she did and cared for her when she was ill like any daughter would. So, when I was experiencing health challenges because of chronic stress, I had to do something! The safety net and security I had in Miss Yemi was not there to come up with a formulation just for me. I prayed and sought how to change my circumstances. What could I do to make it better? Or at minimum different.

The circumstances in my life weren't changing so the only thing I had control of changing was myself. One place I always found solace in was my kitchen. Sometimes it was the only place I could fully express myself. I was preparing something in the kitchen one day and the formula for a hibiscus-based tea came to me. From the moment I sat down and sipped on this tea, my soul was soothed. With every sip, I felt a sense of calm and ease come over me and the tension began to melt away little by little. Thus, Release Recharge Tea was born!

This led to the creation of FREEALITEA with teas to help induce a state of relaxation and facilitate the release of stress and toxicity. I knew if I could experience this state of calm for just a moment every day with something as simple and natural as tea, I could help others do the same. Each cup created a me-time moment for me and a stress-FREE reality.

The recipes in this book feature the leveled-up version of some of FREEALITEA's most popular blends: Who would ever imagine cooking with teas?

In this book, we'll go on a journey together of how to use the plant technology of herbs and herbal tea blends to create tonics and cocktails that will lift your mood, soothe your mind, and help your health.

As you explore this book and open your mind to new possibilities, allow each recipe to create a moment that is just for you. A moment that you too can create a healthy and stress-FREE reality, one cup at a time.

CHAPTER 2 TONICS

Per Oxford's Dictionary, a tonic is:

a medicinal substance taken to give a feeling of vigor or well-being.

something with an invigorating effect.

It can be anything invigorating physically, mentally, or morally.

The body is like a small ecosystem unto itself, and everything is balanced just right.

When some part of the body becomes unbalanced, herbs can be used to help

restore balance or homeostasis. When used appropriately, we can have a deliciously divine herbal preparation that helps invigorates us body, mind, and soul.

Herbal tonics can be used for almost every system in the body.

When preparing a tonic, the parts of herbs used may be the leaves flowers or the roots. Some of you who may be the adventurous type, may try to forage (gather) your own from a nearby wooded area. In theory, that is a fantastic idea. In Native Indigenous American culture, it is believed that the medicine you need grows near you. Consult someone trained in herbology before attempting this. Only certain parts of a plant are safe to use medicinally. For example, the berries of a plant may be toxic while the root has medicinal benefits.

We'll specifically cover herbal tonics for digestion system and relaxation to de-stress.

Herbs for Digestion

My top two herbs that I love to use for the digestive system are ginger and mint.

Ginger

Ginger is a root because it comes from the ground. It is known to help with simple indigestion such as gas. If you eat a meal that you know typically results in gas (why would you do that?), you can drink a cup of ginger tea after to help alleviate the gas. Research has shown that ginger can help certain digestive enzymes work more efficiently. Enzymes are our body's chemicals that break down food substances for us to digest it and absorb the beneficial nutrients. Ginger also may help increase movement of digesting food through the digestive tract.

Remember, better out than in. So, every time you eat, you should eliminate pretty quickly. The rule of thumb is you should eliminate the same amount of times you eat per day.

Ginger also helps relieve nausea. For people experiencing nausea from chemotherapy or morning sickness with pregnancy, ginger can offer some relief. Of note, there are very few herbs that are safe to take during pregnancy. Ginger is one of them.

Peppermint contains menthol, which helps stimulate the intestines. It also helps relax the muscles in the digestive tract, promoting burping. You can eat peppermint candy or mints, which are helpful (Do you always notice the peppermint candies at restaurants?) Peppermint tea is also a great way to take peppermint. You can drink 1–2 cups of tea after a meal to aid digestion.

Before I had major surgery, I prepared the digestive relief tonic to take with me to the hospital. A common side effect of general anesthesia is nausea, vomiting gas, and bloating. Imagine, having abdominal surgery with stitches and staples and putting extra strain and pressure on those areas? Drinking the digestive relief tonic after the surgery prevented nausea and relieved the bloating from surgery. It was delicious and soothing. Something I really needed after a surgical cut that went through many layers of skin, fat, and muscle in my lower abdomen.

Other herbs I love to use for digestive tonics are fennel, yarrow, dandelion root, slippery elm, and aloe.

Digestive Relief Tonic

INGREDIENTS

2 tbsp of dried peppermint leaves

2-3 inches of fresh ginger root peeled and cut

2 ¼ cup of Spring or Distilled Water

Honey

INSTRUCTIONS

Add water and ginger root to a saucepan.

Cover and bring to a boil and allow a rolling boil for 3 minutes

Turn off heat and add dried peppermint

Allow to steep for 15 minutes

Strain and add honey to taste

Cleanse & Calm Tonic

INGREDIENTS

2 ½ cups of Apple Cider

1 Cinnamon Stick

3 Cloves (whole)

2-3 inches of Fresh Ginger Root

INSTRUCTIONS

Place ALL ingredients in a saucepan and cover.

Bring to a boil and allow to boil for 2-3 minutes

Remove from heat

Drink and enjoy warm!

Cleanse & Calm Cocktail

INGREDIENTS

All of the ingredients in the Cleanse & Calm Tonic

Wild Orange Essential Oil

1-2 oz. of Rum (I prefer Caribbean Rum. Babancourt Haitian Rum is my favorite)

INSTRUCTIONS

Use same ingredients and follow instructions to prepare the Cleanse & Calm Tonic.

Strain and add tonic to a spirit glass

Add 1 drop of essential oil

Add rum

Mix and ENJOY!

Cleanse & Calm Simple Syrup

INGREDIENTS

All of the ingredients in the Cleanse & Calm Tonic

INSTRUCTIONS

Place all ingredients into a saucepan with the lid OFF

Cook on high heat at a rolling boil until the tonic thickens.

Once it thickens to your desired consistency, remove from heat

Place in a glass jar like a Mason Jar for storage in a refrigerator

***NOTE Using this simple syrup is a DELICIOUS and healthier alternative to candied yams.

Boils sweet potatoes or yams. Once cooked, drizzle and mix in Cleanse and Calm Tonic syrup

***NOTE Using this simple syrup is a DELICIOUS and healthier alternative to candied yams. Boils sweet potatoes or yams. Once cooked, drizzle and mix in Cleanse and Calm Tonic syrup

Herbs for Relaxation

In May of 2021, my father was diagnosed with laryngeal (throat) cancer. The recommendation was to completely remove his vocal cords. In my nuclear family, my father and I are the only ones who are still living. My brother committed suicide at the age of 21 and my mother died from metastatic breast cancer 14 years ago. Knowing that my purpose is a healing helper, I dropped everything and went to him. I put my house on the market, packed everything, and moved from New Orleans to be with him in Indianapolis. Thankfully, we got a second opinion, and he was able to avoid surgery and be treated with chemo and radiation, but he was unable to eat by mouth for 3 months. For 4 months I put my business FREEALITEA on the back burner to go with my Daddy to every chemo treatment, doctor's appointment, and hospital stay. The nutritionist recommended Glucerna and Ensure for his tube feedings. Not for my Daddy! I wanted him to have the best and give him the highest quality of nourishment to help his body heal. I juiced, prepared herbal tonics, and made ALL of his nutrition with real and whole foods for his feeding tube. The blender and I had a close relationship! It was one of the most stressful times of my life! To make it through those 4 months, I had to practice what I preached and make FREEALITEA a daily ritual to keep my mood and emotions from plummeting. My daily ritual was:

Wake up, give thanks for a new day

Brew my tea. I would choose my blend depending on my intention for the day.

Go outside and put my bare feet on the grass facing the sun. Take 3 deep breaths and touch my toes

Prepare juices and tonics for my Daddy's feeding tube for the day.

Most often I chose blends that would help relax me. The overwhelming stress affected my sleep (only getting 3-4 hours/night), my eating habits, and my muscles were super tense. But once again, if only for a moment, I found solace and an escape from the situation in my cup of tea.

Some of my favorite relaxing herbs are ashwagandha, holy basil, lemon balm, and rosemary.

Mindset & Mood Tonic

INGREDIENTS

3 tbsp of fresh OR 1 ½ tbsp of dried Rosemary

2 Lemons

2 cups of spring water

Honey, agave or stevia to taste (optional)

INSTRUCTIONS

Juice the two lemons and set juice aside

Place water in a saucepan, cover and bring the water to a boil. Once at a rolling boil, turn off heat.

Add rosemary to the saucepan and allow to steep for 10 minutes

Add honey to taste and lemon juice to a mug and stir to mix.

Strain rosemary from the water and add tonic to the lemon and honey mixture.

Stir to mix thoroughly and ENJOY

Mindset & Mood Foot Tonic

INGREDIENTS

Ingredients for Mindset & Mood tonic

Dried lavender buds

Sea Salt and/or Himalayan Pink Salt

INSTRUCTIONS

Triple the amount of ingredients for the Mindset and Mood Tonic.

Follow the instructions to make the tonic but DO NOT STRAIN the rosemary

Add the rosemary tonic and lemon juice to a small tub that your feet will fit in comfortably

Add the lavender and salt

Once the water has cooled to a comfortable temperature, place your feet in the tub, soak, sip, and soothe your tension and troubles away

*OPTIONAL add the petals of your favorite flowers

Mindset & Mood Aromatherapy

INGREDIENTS

Ingredients for the Mindset & Mood Tonic

*OPTIONAL Essential oil such as geranium, ylang ylang, or orange.

INSTRUCTIONS

Prepare Mindset & Mood tonic as described above.

Once water has boiled, add rosemary, lemon, and any essential oils you may want.

Turn off heat

Add to a diffuser to fill your room with the aroma, Breathe intentional deep breaths

OR

Cover your head with a towel over the pot and inhale the aroma.

*NOTES

Aromatherapy stimulates the part of the brain connected to smell, including the nose and the brain.

As molecules that enter the nose through inhalation and reach the brain, they affect an area of the brain, which is linked to the emotions, the heart rate, blood pressure, breathing, memory, stress, and hormone balance. In this way aromatherapy can help with stress and induce a feeling of relaxation. Rosemary is an awesome herb both internally and externally. Just smelling the herb has been found to lower cortisol levels (our stress hormone), and can improve a person's concentration performance, speed, and accuracy.

CHAPTER 3 SMOOTHIES

The Darker the Berry, the Sweeter the Juice

I absolutely LOVE berries. They are so healthy for you and full of antioxidants. Antioxidants are what are known as phytonutrients or natural plant compounds that help reduce oxidative stress. Now I know that is a lot of science but let me tell you WHY it is important to reduce oxidative stress. Oxidative stress produces something called free radicals that can damage cells and contribute to chronic diseases such as heart disease, cancer and diabetes. There are many different antioxidants to include vitamins A, C, E, and anthocyanins found in dark colored berries.

It's amazing how just doing something fun can be such a healthy and wealthy experience. Growing up, we used to spend summers at Fox Lake in Angola, Indiana. My grandparents purchased a small 2-bedroom 1 bath cottage that overlooks the lake. Nowadays, parents scramble to find fulfilling and educational summer camps. My summers were spent swimming in the lake all day, every day that it didn't rain, catching lightning bugs with my cousins and occasionally fishing with Paw Paw. On some of those days, my grandmother, affectionately known as "Nanny", would take me and my girl cousins to pick berries. We didn't go to a berry farm, we picked wild berries that grew in various locations around Fox Lake resort. And she knew exactly where the wild strawberries, raspberries, and mulberries grew. I even remember an apple tree that grew by an old-abandoned house. Nanny would say, "OK girls, you want to go pick berries?" She gave us a little bag and we would walk hand in hand swinging our arms singing, "Here we go to and fro, to and fro here we go." I can still feel the softness and warmth of Nanny's hand as we walked down the lane singing, laughing and swinging our arms. Now if you know anything about foraging for food, then you know you need to find a lot of it in order to have a full meal. Especially when we were feeding at minimum 2 adults and 3 children. It's not like going to the market to pick up a pint or two of strawberries and voila. We might find 15 wild raspberries at the most or 10 strawberries. Nanny would take all that we had picked and make a berry cobbler. Let me tell you, you have NEVER tasted a cobbler like this! All of this fresh vine ripened berries sweetened with sugar and Nanny's love stirred into a light, buttery and flaky homemade piecrust – it truly tasted like manna from heaven! At 50 years of age, I treasure those moments so much! To this day I can still taste the sweetness of those berry cobblers. I think every time I make a Berry Blast Stress-FREE smoothie or the Royal Berry Blast, I will say Nanny's name out loud and bring the memory of her presence close to me.

Smoothies are a quick and easy way to intake nutrients especially on-the-go. The beauty of smoothies is that you maintain the fiber content unlike juices. Tea Smoothies are AMAZING! Instead of using plain water to blend, use your favorite tea for added flavor and benefits. You get more bang for your buck in vitamins and nutrients by combining the two. Let's explore the different flavors with these tea smoothie recipes.

Royal Berry Blast

INGREDIENTS

Handful of Blueberries

Handful of Strawberries/Raspberries

Handful of Blackberries (optional)

1 ½ cup of Release Your RoyalTEA, brewed

INSTRUCTIONS

Combine ingredients in a blender.

Sweeten to taste

Release & Relieve Turmeric Smoothie

INGREDIENTS

2 cups of Release & Relieve Tea

1 handful of leafy greens (spinach, kale etc.)

1 kiwi

½ mango

INSTRUCTIONS

Boil 2 ¼ cups of water. Once boiled, add 2 tbsp. of Release & Relieve tea.

Steep and let cool. Once cooled, strain tea and set aside

Place a handful of leafy greens in a blender. Add tea and blend

Strain pulp from liquid. Add green liquid back to the blender

Add 1 kiwi and ½ of a mango to blender and blend

*Optional add honey or another sweetener to taste

It's Easy to Be Green

Growing up, The Muppets were some of my favorite characters. I used to watch The Muppet show every week. My favorites were Fozzie Bear and Miss Piggy. Kermit was cool too. Some of you may remember the song Kermit the Frog used to sing called, "It's Not Easy Being Green."

It's not easy bein' green

It seems you blend in

With so many other ordinary things...

But green's the color of spring

And green can be cool and friendly like

And green can be big like a mountain

Or important like a river or tall like a tree...

And Kermit is right, green is cool and friendly and important!

When I was young my grandmother used to tell me, "Michelle, you have to eat your green vegetables every day. It's important to keep you regular."

As I have learned more and more about health and evolved on this wellness journey, I've discovered all kinds of cool green options that make it easy to be green.

One that I keep in my arsenal is green tea.

There are over 20 varieties of green tea. It depends on the type of plant grown, the region it is grown in and when the leaves are harvested.

Five of the most popular are Sencha, Matcha, Genmaicha, Bancha, and Gyokuro.

Sencha

Sencha is the most popular green tea in Japan. It is one whose leaves are first harvested in the spring; therefore, it contains the most nutrients. That is why it was chosen as one of the main ingredients in FREEALITEA's Release & Purify Green Tea. Even though it is a green tea, when brewed, it is a light-yellow color.

Matcha

Matcha is actually powdered green tea. What makes it different is how it is grown, processed, and prepared. Approximately 20-30 days before harvested, the plant is covered with cloths to block the sunlight. Then the entire plant to include leaves and stems are picked at the first harvest. Blocking the sunlight from the plants increases chlorophyll production which deepens the flavor and the nutrient content. The leaves and stems are then ground to a fine powder. When prepared, it results in a beautiful rich green color. Because of how it is grown, matcha has approximately three times the caffeine amount than sencha green. However, it doesn't result in the buzz and jittery feeling with a crash that coffee typically does. Though the caffeine content is substantial, while keeping you alert and on point, it also has a calming effect. Though you are alert, you also feel relaxed, calm, and stress-less.

Moringa

Moringa leaves come from a tree native to India. However, moringa does grow here in America. I have seen a tree in Florida and my line sister has one growing at her home in Houston. It also grows in Africa, Caribbean islands, and South America. It is also known as the "drumstick tree, the Ben oil tree, and the Horseradish tree. This herb has grown popular in recent years due to the discovery by the masses of its rich nutrient profile.

It is known as the "king of herbs" which has been used for centuries for its medicinal uses and incorporated in meals. Some of its traditional uses are for anemia, high blood pressure, anxiety, chest congestion, and skin ailments.

This power-packed plant is a rich source of nutrients that you would not think of in plants.

Dried moringa leaves contain:

12Xs the amount of Vitamin C in oranges

4Xs the amount of protein than eggs

25Xs the amount of iron than spinach

15Xs the amount of potassium than bananas

10Xs the amount of Vitamin A than carrots

17Xs the amount of calcium than milk

Having grown up Indianapolis, I wasn't familiar with moringa. But once I found it, it was a game-changer for me! Being a vegetarian, rich sources of protein that didn't come from something with a mama or four legs was important to me. People always say, "How do you get your protein?" We've been sold a wooden nickel that you can only be healthy and have a full and whole diet by incorporating meat and dairy. By looking at this rich nutrient profile, now you see why they call it the "King of herbs" and this Queen had to use it in two of the FREEaliTEA blends.

Green tea, specifically sencha is important to me for a different reason. When my Daddy was going through treatment for grade 2 laryngeal (throat) cancer, it got to a point where he didn't and couldn't eat and was tired from the radiation. Though he was 76 years old at the time, he still lived a full life working full time driving an 18-wheeler truck. Driving that big truck was a place of peace and power for my Daddy. Without that, I feared he would just slip away. Before his treatment began, they placed a g-tube (gastric tube/feeding tube) so he could still get nutrients. At that point, every calorie and pound counted. So, one day after his radiation treatment, we did a little shopping at Costco. One moment we were good and walking around, the next he was fatigued and didn't feel like doing anything. It happened in a matter of minutes. Often during this process of caring for my Daddy I often felt helpless. How could I be a Physician, a Healing Helper and not help my own Daddy?!

Then it came to me. I had something in my Farmacy arsenal that could help. I prayed about it and waited to hear from God. The answer was moringa and sencha. Green tea is known to have anti-cancer properties. Because of that and the calming-energizing effect it has, I paired it with the moringa for the nutrients and voila! I knew the taste wasn't going to be pleasant and we didn't have time to wait for him to slip slowly and possibly waste it. I brewed a cup of the two herbs together and placed it right in his g-tube. His energy level started to return and after four days of doing this, he returned to work.

*Disclaimer I don't recommend anyone do this unless you have checked with YOUR doctor. Since I am a doctor and caring for my Daddy, I made an educated and intuitive decision with great results.

The moral of the story is it is easy being green. When you put the right greens in you on a consistent basis, as Kermit the Frog told us, it's "important like a river or tall like a tree…"

Purify Green Dream Juice

INGREDIENTS

Release & Purify Green Tea (brewed and chilled)

1 stalk of Celery

2-3 leaves of Lacinato Kale

Juice of ½ lemon

Honey or agave

Distilled water

INSTRUCTIONS

Heat 10 ounces of water to 150 – 180 degrees. Add ½ tablespoon of Release & Purify Green Tea.

Let steep for 5 minutes. Remove loose tea and allow chill in refrigerator for 45 minutes – 1 hour.

Add ½ of the chilled tea to a blender. Add 1 stalk of celery and kale leaves cleaned and cut up to easily blend. Blend. Strain through a sifter. Add honey to taste and lemon juice. Stir and ENJOY!

Purify & Pineapple Smoothie

INGREDIENTS

Release & Purify Green Tea (brewed & chilled)

½ - ¾ cup of Pineapple Chunks

1 Kiwi, peeled

Juice of 1 Lemon

2 Kale Leaves

Distilled Water

INSTRUCTIONS

Heat water to no hotter than 170 degrees. Add ½ tablespoon of Release & Purify Green Tea. Steep for 4 minutes. Remove tea bag or diffuser. Allow to chill.

Add all ingredients to include chilled Release & Purify Green Tea in a blender

Blend until smooth

Add more tea or water, if necessary, to desired consistency

Optional add honey to taste

Stress FREELIFE Smoothie

INGREDIENTS

1 handful of spinach, kale or Swiss chard

1 green apple

½ avocado

Juice of 1 lime

Juice of 1 lemon

14 oz. of fresh spring water

Honey to taste

*Dash of cayenne pepper optional

INSTRUCTION

Core and slice apples

Blend with water and (strain if you desire a thinner consistency or may juice apples in a juicer)

Use ¼ to ½ of an avocado depending on desired consistency

Blend remaining ingredients together and sweeten to taste

May add a pinch of cayenne for an extra kick

Berry Blast Stress-FREE Smoothie

INGREDIENTS

½ cup strawberries

½ cup blueberries

½ avocado

Handful of spinach

1 cup of almond milk

1 tsp. cinnamon

Dash of pure vanilla extract

INSTRUCTIONS

Place ALL ingredients in blender except avocado with fresh spring water or almond milk

Add ¼ to ½ of an avocado depending on desired consistency and blend

Blend remaining ingredients together and sweeten to taste with honey or agave.

Chocolate Smoothie

INGREDIENTS

¾ cup water

4 Medjool dates, pitted

¼ avocado

1 heaping tablespoons cacao powder

½ teaspoon vanilla extract

1 handful fresh baby spinach (optional)

1 heaping cup ice cubes

INSTRUCTIONS

In a high-speed blender, combine the water, dates, avocado, cacao powder, vanilla, and spinach, if using, and blend until very smooth. Taste the pudding-like mixture to make sure there's enough sweetness and chocolate flavor to your liking and adjust anything to your taste. (Keep in mind that the flavor will be diluted a bit more once you add the ice.)

Add the ice and blend again, until the smoothie has more of a milkshake-like texture. You can add as much ice as needed to achieve the texture you want, but keep in mind that extra ice will dilute the chocolate flavor. Serve right away.

*If you are a fan of bananas, may add ¼ of a banana or substitute banana for avocado

Citrus Rise & Shine

INGREDIENTS

Juice of 5 Oranges

Juice of 2 grapefruits

Juice of 4 lemons

Juice of 4 limes

½ inch of Ginger Root

1 1/3 cup of Spring Water – separated 1 cup and 1/3 cup

Honey to taste

*¼ tsp. Apple Cider Vinegar optional

INSTRUCTIONS

In 1/3 cup of spring water, blend ginger root. Strain and set liquid aside.

Add all fresh-squeezed juices in a pitcher

Add 1 cup of spring water

Add ginger juice

Add honey to taste if necessary

Stir and enjoy

Release, Rise & Island Shine Smoothie

INGREDIENTS

1 ½ cup of Release, Rise & Shine tea, brewed

½ - ¾ cup Pineapple (in chunks)

½ Mango

INSTRUCTIONS

Add all ingredients in a blender

Blend until smooth

Add more tea or water, if necessary, to desired consistency

Optional add honey to taste

Chill & Chai Warm Smoothie

INGREDIENTS

1½ cups hot brewed Release Chill & Chai

½ cup coconut milk

¼ inch chunk ginger, grated or finely chopped

½ Tbs. raw honey

½ tsp cinnamon

½ cup of Rum Cream or other cream liqueur such as Irish Cream, or Bourbon Cream.

INSTRUCTIONS

Blend all non-alcoholic ingredients together. Can enjoy this as a warm tea smoothie.

Or add cream liqueur, shake or stir to enjoy the G & G version.

CHAPTER 4 TAILS
– Mocktails or the G & G version

Release Your ImmuniTEA Tail

INGREDIENTS

¼ cup of Release Your ImmuniTEA simple syrup (you can add less or more depending on your preference)

1 cup of Caribbean rum (I prefer Babancourt Haitian rum)

Juice from 1 fresh squeezed lime

One handful of blackberries

3-5 mint sprigs

*Optional tonic water

INSTRUCTIONS

Muddle the blackberries

Combine syrup, rum blackberries, mint leaves, and lime juice in a cocktail shaker. Stir (or shake) and strain into a glass over ice.

Top off with a small amount of tonic water if tastes too sweet

Immune Berry Spritzer

INGREDIENTS

1 handful of blueberries

1 handful of blackberries

1 handful of raspberries (optional)

honey or another sweetener such as agave

20 oz. of distilled or spring water

2 Tablespoons of Release YOUR ImmuniTEA

2 cups of Release Your ImmuniTEA Tea brewed, chilled

Club Soda/Pellegrino etc.

INSTRUCTIONS

Bring 20 ounces of water to a boil. Add 2 tablespoons of Release Your ImmuniTEA. Allow to steep for at least 10 minutes. Strain and sweeten to taste with honey/agave etc. Chill in the refrigerator for at least 1 hour.

In a glass add the berries. Using a wooden spoon or muddler, muddle the berries.

Add Release Your ImmuniTEA to glass about 2/3 full.

Pour back and forth between two glasses to adequately mix or use a cocktail shaker

Top with ice if desired.

Top off with a splash of club soda/ Pellegrino etc.

***OPTIONAL Make it a G&G (Good & Grown) spritzer by adding 2 ounces of your favorite gin (but don't sin)

Makes 2 servings

Berries & Bubbles

INGREDIENTS

2 cups of Release Your ImmuniTEA, brewed and sweetened to taste

Blueberry Moscato

Vodka

Rose Prosecco

INSTRUCTIONS

Brew Release Your ImmuniTEA. Sweeten and allow to cool and/or chill in refrigerator to desired temperature

Mix Release Your ImmuniTEA, blueberry Moscato, and vodka in a picture. Stir

Pour into a chilled glass.

Top off with Rose Prosecco to desired amount

CHEERS!

Release Romance ChocolaTEAni

8 oz. of Release Romance Tea brewed

4 oz. Bailey's Irish Cream

4 oz. Vodka

INSTRUCTIONS

Combine Release Romance Tea, Baileys, and vodka in a large cocktail shaker. Fill with ice and shake until thoroughly chilled, about 20 seconds. Divide evenly between glasses.

Optional: Drizzle with chocolate either in or out of the glass.

Enjoy and release your romance!

Royale RoyalTEA

INGREDIENTS

¼ cup of Release Your Royal TEA brewed and sweetened if desired

1 oz. Chambord

6 ounces chilled dry Champagne

INSTRUCTIONS

Pour Release Your RoyalTEA to a Champagne flute

Add the Chambord

While holding the glass at a 45-degree angle (this helps preserve the bubbles), gently pour in the Champagne.

Garnish with a raspberry, if desired.

Serve immediately, TOAST and ENJOY!

*NOTES

One bottle of Champagne will make approximately 5 drinks. One small (375 mL) bottle of Chambord is enough for 25 drinks. So, you'll need five times as much Champagne as Chambord.

RoyalTEANI

INGREDIENTS

8 cups water

8 tbsp of Release Your RoyalTEA

Honey or ½ -1 cup granulated sugar

1 ½ cups Chambord Liquor optional

½ cup good quality Vodka. I prefer Grey Goose

Mint springs, Raspberries, Oranges, etc. for garnish

INSTRUCTIONS

Bring water to a boil then remove from the heat.

Add Release Your RoyalTEA, cover and let steep for 10 minutes.

Add honey or sugar stir until mixed thoroughly. Strain and allow the tea cool.

Add in Chambord and Vodka if desired

Pour into ice-filled glasses.

Garnish with a mint sprig, raspberries, oranges, whatever you love.

ENJOY!!

Royal Carnival

Mardi Gras or Carnival season is a time to celebrate life to the fullest. It is an opportunity to "do whatcha wanna" and dance and drink your cares away. There is NO JUDGEMENT during Mardi Gras. You will see anything and EVERYTHING in the street. But it is so much fun! I I always release my inner child and just be free! Because New Orleans doesn't have an open container law, you can go to parties, balls, and parades and bring your special cocktail with you. Not in a glass, but what is called, "a go-cup". Some of the coveted "throws" or items thrown from the parade floats, are signature plastic cups. Perfect to fill and refill as needed to keep the good times rollin'!

This FREEALITEA cocktail is an ode to New Orleans Carnival season.

Laissez Les Bon Temps Rouler!

INGREDIENTS

2 Tbsp of Release Your Royal TEA

2 cups of Spring of Distilled Water

Handful of Blackberries

4 ounces of Gin

Fresh Basil Leaves

Honey or desired sweetener

Juice of 1 Lime

INSTRUCTIONS

Bring water to a boil then remove from the heat.

Add Release Your RoyalTEA, cover and let steep for 10 minutes.

Add honey or sugar stir until mixed thoroughly. Strain and allow the tea cool.

In a cocktail shaker, muddle blackberries with gin, 4 basil leaves, and lime juice,

Double strain, using a fine-mesh strainer, to remove seeds.

Add Release Your Royal TEA.

Shake well.

Fill 3-4 rock glasses ½ way with ice. Divide cocktail among the glasses.

Garnish with a basil leaf, slice of lime, or blackberry. Or all 3 if you wanna!

R&R Sangria

R&R Sangria

INGREDIENTS

2 oranges, halved and thinly sliced

1 small granny smith apple, core removed and thinly sliced

1 lime, thinly sliced

1-pint raspberries

1-pint blueberries

3 cups of Release Recharge Tea brewed, chilled, and sweetened

½ cup ginger beer

1½ cup red wine

INSTRUCTIONS

Bring 3 ½ cups of water to a boil. Add 3 tablespoons of Release Recharge tea. Allow to steep for at least 10 minutes. Strain and sweeten to taste. Chill in the refrigerator for at least 1 hour.

In a large pitcher, combine oranges, apples, lime slices, and raspberries. Using a wooden spoon, muddle the fruit until there is about ¼ cup of juice

Add Release Recharge tea that has already been brewed,

Stir and mix

Pour into glasses with fruit, about 2/3 full.

Top with ginger beer and serve

Makes 8 servings

*OPTIONAL To enhance the flavor, add a shot of bourbon

Rise & Shine Sangria

INGREDIENTS

1 Orange

1 Lime

½ Lemon

½ Grapefruit (optional)

2 cups Release Rise & Shine Tea brewed, sweetened, and chilled

2 cups of Lemon Moscato

INSTRUCTIONS

Bring 2 ½ cups of water to a boil. Add 2 tablespoons of Release Recharge tea. Allow to steep for at least 10 minutes. Strain and sweeten to taste. Chill in the refrigerator for at least 1 hour.

In a large pitcher, combine oranges, lime slices, lemon, and grapefruit. Using a wooden spoon, muddle the fruit until there is about ¼ cup of juice

Add Release Rise & Shine tea that has already been brewed

Add Moscato

Stir and mix

Pour into glasses with fruit, about 2/3 full.

Makes 6 servings

Rise & Shine Toddy

INGREDIENTS
4 tbsp of Release Rise & Shine Tea

1 (2-inch) piece fresh ginger, peeled and thinly sliced

4 cups of spring water

½ cup of Bourbon

Honey

INSTRUCTIONS
Add fresh ginger to 4 cups of water in a pan. Bring to a boil and let boil for 2 minutes.

Remove pan from heat.

Add Release Rise & Shine tea (Can add tea to empty tea bags or loose in pan). Let steep for 15 minutes.

Using a strainer (or remove tea bags) strain the tea. Add honey to taste and stir

Whisk in bourbon and serve hot or warm.

*OPTIONAL add a dash of cayenne pepper for an extra kick

Release Relieve & Sparkle

For the golden simple syrup:
1 tablespoon of Release Relieve Tea

½ cup of honey

1 cup of water

4 pcs orange zest, wide strips

1 3-inh cinnamon

For the drink:
½ cup fresh squeezed orange juice, chilled

1 bottle Champagne, chilled (can substitute Prosecco or any sparkling wine)

Garnish (optional):

Orange slices

Cinnamon sticks

Edible "glitter"

INSTRUCTIONS

In a medium pot, bring water to a boil. Remove from the heat, add the Release & Relieve tea to the pot. Cover and steep 10-15 minutes.

Strain and add the honey to the pot of tea with the orange zest (if desired). Bring to a boil over high heat. Stir to mix ingredients well.

Boil 3-5 minutes. Reduce heat and simmer 15 – 20 minutes until the liquid starts to thicken.

Turn off heat, cover pot, and allow mixture to cool to room temperature.

Place cooled mixture into the fridge to chill completely; 20 minutes or preferably overnight before using in your cocktail.

To serve:

Run an orange slice around the rim of each champagne flute or any stemmed glass. Place the edible "glitter" into a small plate or dish. Dip and turn the rims of each glass into the sugar. Set aside.

Add about 2 tablespoons each of the orange juice and simple syrup into each glass. Top off each glass with champagne. Garnish with an orange slice or cinnamon stick.

NOTES

*The flavored syrup can be made a few days in advance. Store in an air-tight jar like a mason jar up to 2 weeks.

*For a mocktail, replace the champagne with sparkling white grape, pear, or apple juice.

RootTEAni

INGREDIENTS

6 tbsp of Release & Relieve Tea

6 cups of water

3 cups ice cubes

25 fluid ounces of Vodka

2 cups of Ginger Beer

Honey to taste

INSTRUCTIONS

Bring 6 cups of water to a boil. Once has reached the boiling point. Turn off the heat and add tea.

Let steep for 15-30 minutes.

Add honey and stir if desire a sweeter taste

Place in refrigerator to cool

Fill a large glass pitcher or punch bowl about ½ way with ice cubes. Pitcher should hold about two gallons.

Pour in the cooled tea then add the vodka and ginger beer.

Stir it well with a long spoon then set it out to serve in 4-ounce glasses. Guests can add ice to their cup, then serve the punch from the pitcher.

Garnish with mint and lime

Pink Ginger Sunrise

INGREDIENTS

1 Tbsp. Release Rise & Shine Tea

10 oz. of Spring or Distilled Water

Juice of a Pink Grapefruit

½ cup of Ginger Beer

Honey to taste

INSTRUCTIONS

Boil Water. Remove from heat

Add Release Rise & Shine Tea steep for 10 minutes

Strain

Sweeten with honey to taste

Chill in refrigerator

Once chilled, add grapefruit juice, stir and pour into ice-filled glasses

Top with ginger beer

OPTIONAL

To make this a G & G drink, add your favorite spirit such as rum or vodka

Fancy FREETEAni

INGREDIENTS

Release & Purify Green Tea (brewed and chilled)

Tito's vodka

Lime

Distilled Water

INSTRUCTIONS

Heat 16 ounces of water to 150 – 180 degrees. Add 1 tablespoons of Release & Purify Green Tea. Allow to steep for at least 5 minutes. Strain and sweeten to taste with honey/agave etc. Chill in the refrigerator for at least 1 hour.

Once the tea has chilled, in a fresh glass, add 1 ounce of Tito's and 1 cup of Release & Purify Green tea.

Cut a lime wedge and squeeze fresh juice.

CHEERS!

CHAPTER 5 SOUPS & SALADS

Fall Harvest Salad

INGREDIENTS

2 Green Apples

2 Pears

1 Stalk of Celery

Leafy Greens (Romaine, Green Leaf etc.)

INSTRUCTIONS

Break lettuce into small bite size pieces.

Line on the bottom of plate or bowl. Set aside

In a separate bowl, cut apples, pears and celery into bite size pieces leaving the skin on.

Stir in Apple Cider Vinaigrette until evenly distributed.

Garnish with chopped parsley (optional)

Purification Breakfast

INGREDIENTS

1-2 Oranges

1-2 Kiwi

Romaine Lettuce

Golden Raisins

*OPTIONAL Release & Relieve simple syrup

INSTRUCTIONS

Soak raisins minimum 8 hours in spring water until they plump. Store in an airtight container in the refrigerator.

Break romaine into bite size pieces and arrange in a small bowl.

Peel and cut orange and kiwi

Place orange, kiwi on top of romaine lettuce.

Place a few spoonsful of golden raisins on top of orange and kiwi mixture.

OPTIONAL pour some of the juice from raisins or drizzle a small amount of Release & Relieve simple syrup.

*NOTES

Can quick soak the raisins by bringing a small amount of water to boil. Pour over golden raisins, just enough to cover them. Wait about an hour for them to plump. Then store in an airtight container in the refrigerator between uses.

Full Spectrum Stress Release Salad with Release Recharge Vinaigrette

INGREDIENTS

1 tangerine or satsuma

Cherry tomatoes, halved

1 Avocado sliced

1/3 cup Basil leaves

1 ½ cup Romaine lettuce, Green Leaf lettuce or Arugula in bite size pieces

1 cup Baby Spinach

Release Recharge Vinaigrette

INSTRUCTIONS

Build salad starting with the base of leafy greens (romaine, green leaf, and/or arugula)

Mix in spinach

Add cherry tomatoes, tangerine slices, cherries, avocado, and basil leaves

Mix in Release Recharge Vinaigrette

May season with sea salt or other desired seasonings

*OPTIONAL Add feta cheese, cucumber, and/or almond slices

FREEALITAL Stew

INGREDIENTS

2 cups pumpkin or butternut squash, chopped

1 medium-sized carrot, chopped

1 medium sweet potato, chopped

1 green - yellow plantains, chopped

1 small taro or cassava, chopped

1 turnip or parsnip

1 cup of Mirliton (chayote) or Zucchini

1 Red or Orange Bell Pepper

1 handful of Spinach (optional)

2 cups of Coconut Milk

1 ½ cups of Release Relieve Tea (brewed)

1 cup of Water

4 sprigs of fresh Thyme

¼ cup of Cilantro, chopped

1 Red Onion, chopped

2 Scallions, chopped into large pieces

3-7 Garlic Cloves (depending on taste)

1 large tomato, chopped

2 Bay Leaves

Bragg's Liquid Aminos (optional)

1 tsp. Curry Powder

6 Pimento Berries (allspice) or ground allspice

Scotch Bonnet Pepper (can substitute fresh chili pepper or habanero)

Pink Salt or Sea Salt (optional)

INSTRUCTIONS

Prepare the Release Relieve tea Bring 1 ½ cups of water to a boil. Once the water has boiled, turn off the heat and add 1 ½ tablespoon of Release Relieve tea. Steep for 10 – 15 minutes. Then strain

Add the tea coconut milk, and water into a large saucepan and bring to a boil.

Once the liquid has reached boiling point reduce the heat to medium then add the scallion, tomato, thyme, coriander/cilantro, onion, garlic. pimento berries and bay leaves.

Taste and add any additional seasonings according to your taste

Simmer for 5 minutes

Add the sweet potato, turnip, cassava root, carrots along with 1 cup of pumpkin and ½ plantain while stirring the saucepan

Add the spices – curry powder, black pepper, salt (if you are using it) and stir once more.

Bring the saucepan to a final rolling boil before reducing the flame to medium/low.

Place a scotch bonnet into the saucepan (DO NOT PRICK unless you want it HOT)

Cover the saucepan and simmer for 25 minutes. After this time you will notice the stew thicken from the vegetables breaking down

Fold in the remaining plantain, pumpkin/butternut squash so they cook evenly.

Cover the saucepan with a lid again and cook the vegetables for 10 minutes.

Add zucchini at this time if you are using it and cook for another 5 minutes until vegetables are soft.

Remove the thyme stems, scotch bonnet, and bay leaves before serving

If you want to add spinach, add a handful at this time while the pot is still hot and stir.

Serve warm

ENJOY!

Release & Purify Green Soup

INGREDIENTS

2 tsps. Of Release & Purify Green Tea

1 tablespoon Extra-virgin Olive Oil (+ extra for drizzling)

½ Small Red Onion (peeled and chopped)

2 Green Onion sprigs

2 Garlic Cloves (minced)

1 tablespoon Ginger (peeled and minced)

½ tsp Turmeric Powder

1 tsp Cumin powder

2 cups Water

2 cups Spinach

1 cup Watercress (chopped)

Bunch of Fresh Cilantro or Parsley, chopped (per your taste)

1 Zucchini, chopped

1 tsp. Sea Salt

Black Pepper (to taste)

Cayenne Pepper (optional)

INSTRUCTIONS

Add 2 teaspoons of Release & Purify Green Tea to a teabag. In a medium saucepan, bring water just before boiling. Remove from heat and add the green tea bag. Let steep for 3 to 4 minutes, and then remove. Set the broth aside.

In a medium size pot over medium high heat, add 1 olive oil and red onion. Sauté for 2-3 minutes, until translucent.

Add garlic, ginger, turmeric, cumin, green onions, and zucchini (leave a little to top bowl at the end) and stir. Sauté for 3 minutes. Stir in sea salt. Turn the heat off.

Add green tea broth, spinach and watercress to the pot and using a hand mixer, blend until smooth. Alternatively, you can transfer all the ingredients to a food processor or blender and blend until smooth.

Divide soup among two bowls. Top with remaining zucchini pieces.

Add a hit of cayenne pepper and/or Black Pepper to taste

Top with chopped cilantro or parsley

Relieve Sweet Potato Soup

INGREDIENTS

1 Tbsp Coconut Oil

4 Shallots or 1 medium red onion

1/4 cup of chopped ginger (peeled)

4 cloves of garlic

1 large, sweet potato peeled and chopped

2 large carrots peeled and chopped

1 Sea Salt

½ tsp Black Pepper

½ tsp. Cayenne Pepper

2 tsp. Curry Powder

1 tsp. Coriander

1 tsp Cumin

1 15 oz. can of Coconut Milk

1 cup of Release & Relieve Tea

1 cup of Vegetable or Chicken Broth

1 cup Baby Spinach

Juice of 1 lime

½ cup of Cilantro, chopped (optional)

1 tablespoon water (optional)

INSTRUCTIONS

Add the coconut oil to a large pot over medium-high heat.

When it melts, add the shallots and let them cook for 3-4 minutes. Add the garlic and ginger and cook for 1 more minute.

Add the sweet potato, carrots, sea salt, black pepper, cayenne. Coriander, curry, and cumin and stir the pot for about 30 seconds.

Add the Release & Relieve tea and stock to the pot and bring the pot to a boil. Reduce the heat to medium and simmer for 10 minutes, or until the vegetables are soft.

Transfer the soup to your blender, add plain Greek yogurt, and blend until smooth.

**For a thicker consistency, may blend all or part of the soup. Then return to the pot.

Add the coconut milk and lime juice, and heat through.

Turn off heat and stir in spinach.

Serve warm and garnish with cilantro if desired

Golden Broccoli Soup

INGREDIENTS

1 Tbsp. Release & Relieve Turmeric Tea

2 Broccoli Crowns cut into pieces

2 Carrots chopped

2 Garlic Cloves, crushed

1 Red Onion chopped small

¾ -1 cup Raw Cashews

4 cups of water

1 Bouillon cube

1 tsp Curry Powder

1 tsp Smoked Paprika

Black Pepper

½ Tbsp Bragg's Liquid Aminos

Salt and pepper to taste or other seasoning to taste. I often add Tony Chachere's herb seasoning.

Olive Oil for cooking

INSTRUCTIONS

Boil 1 cup of water. Once has reached a boil, turn off heat. Add 1 tablespoon of Release & Relieve tea. Allow to steep for at least 5 minutes. Set aside.

Heat 1-2 tbsp of olive oil in a soup pot over low to medium heat. Cook onions and carrots for about 5-7 minutes, until soft. Add salt, black pepper, and curry, Bragg's and smoked paprika and mix well. Heat for about 1 minute longer.

Add broccoli pieces and cook about 5 minutes longer.

Add Release & Relieve tea, 3 cups of water, and bouillon cube. Bring to a boil, and then reduce to a simmer.

Add garlic

Cook for 5-7 minutes, until vegetables are tender.

Place cashews in a blender, add enough soup liquid (just liquid, no veggies) to cover cashews. Carefully blend cashews into a smooth paste, adding more liquid if needed.

Add cashew mixture back into the soup. Mix well, and warm through. You may add moe turmeric according to your taste.

**OPTIONAL I like to garnish the finished product with fresh cilantro and a swirl of siracha sauce.

Other options may be fresh basil and a hit of cayenne pepper if you want to heat it up Release & Relieve Tea

Rise Caribbean Black Bean Soup

INGREDIENTS

29 oz. can of Black Beans

2 Carrots

1 red Bell Pepper

1 Onion

3 stalks of Green Onions

2 Roma Tomatoes

1 Green Plantain

3 cloves of Garlic

1 cup Coconut Milk

1 tsp. Turmeric

1 tsp. Curry

1 tsp. Allspice

Smoked Paprika

1 Bouillon Cube

3 springs of Fresh Thyme

3 Black Peppercorns

1 Scotch Bonnet Pepper

1 cup of Release Rise & Shine tea, brewed

1 ¾ - 2 cups of water

1 Bay Leaf

Olive oil

Sea Salt (optional)

INSTRUCTIONS

Chop onions, tomatoes, 3 cloves of garlic, bell pepper, and green onion

Peel and slice green plantain in small to medium size pieces.

Rinse and drain black beans to remove all residue and extra salt

Sauté onion, tomatoes, 3 cloves of garlic, thyme, black pepper and green onions in olive oil on medium heat until onion is translucent (approximately 3 minutes)

Increase heat, then add black beans, bouillon cube, bell pepper, carrots, plantain, and all seasonings.

Add water and bring to a boil.

Cover and reduce heat to a simmer. Let cook for about 25 minutes or more until plantains are tender and soup has a creamy consistency.

Add coconut milk. Stir and let simmer for approximately 10 more minutes. Taste and add more seasonings if necessary.

Remove from heat

Serve in bowl and garnish with cilantro.

Can serve with rice and/or avocado.

CHAPTER 6 SWEETS

Most of us are addicted to sugar. My addiction started very early in childhood. My grandfather affectionately known as Paw Paw absolutely LOVED sweets! Because of her love for him, my grandmother affectionately known as Nanny, gave him what he loved. Every dinner had a dessert. And not just any dessert, it was always something homemade. Pound cake, yellow cake with caramel icing, apple pie, peach cobbler, chess pie… Oh my goodness, I'm salivating just thinking about it! And everything was made from scratch! Sweets bring back happy memories. It's no wonder it is one of my comfort foods when I feel extremely stressed. The sweetness temporarily makes a bitter situation seem sweeter. Until my body says, "Whoa, you are 50 not 5!" To balance things out, I had to create a way to satisfy those cravings a healthier way. This chapter is dedicated to my grandmother, Martha Louise Black Jackson AKA Nanny. One of the sweetest and brightest beings I have ever known. Who made sure before she left this world to go to the next, that I knew the secret behind her light and flaky pie crust and buttery rolls.

Romance ChocolaTEA Truffles

Ingredients

1 can full-fat coconut milk (unsweetened)

10 oz dark or milk chocolate chips chocolate

3 tablespoons of Release Romance ChocolaTEA

2 tbsp coconut oil

½ tsp. of Vanilla Extract (optional)

5-6 softened pitted Medjool dates (if using unsweetened chocolate)

Instructions

To prepare dates, bring 2 cups of water to a boil and pour over dates in a small bowl. Let sit for 10 minutes.

In a small saucepan heat coconut milk, coconut oil, softened dates**, and Release Romance ChocolATEA over medium to high heat. Simmer for about 5 minutes over low. Strain through a sieve and pour back into the saucepan.

Add chocolate and keep over low heat. Stir occasionally until chocolate has fully melted and everything is combined. DO NOT ALLOW CHOCOLATE TO BURN* Add sweetener (maple syrup) if needed.

Transfer into an airtight bowl and refrigerate for about 3-4 hours or overnight.

Take 1 tbsp of the chocolate mixture and form into little truffle balls with the palms of your hands.

Repeat until all mixture is gone.

ENJOY and store leftovers in an airtight container in the refrigerator for up to 2 weeks.

Optional: Roll in cocoa, cacao, sprinkles, or other topping you might like.

NOTES

*Right before serving, roll truffles in a bowl of dark cocoa or cacao powder, tossing to coat. Remove from the bowl with fingers or a fork, tapping to remove excess

**Squeeze out any excess liquids before adding them into the coconut milk.

Raw Berry Crisp with Cashew Cream and Release Your ImmuniTEA Glaze

INGREDIENTS

Raw Berry Crisp:

6 cups fresh berries

1 cup pecans

1 cup walnuts

1 Tbsp. Pure Maple Syrup or Honey

½ tsp. Cinnamon

1 cup Medjool dates (pitted)

Cashew Cream:

1 cup cashews (soaked)

5 Medjool dates (pitted)

2 tsp. vanilla extract

¾ - 1 ¼ cup of water

INSTRUCTIONS

Berry Crisp

In a (7- x 11-inch) dish, toss berries with maple syrup.

Put pecans, walnuts, dates and cinnamon into a food processor and pulse until coarsely ground.

Scatter nut mixture over berries and serve immediately, or chill until ready to serve.

Cashew Cream

Combine all ingredients, start with only ¾ cup water, and blend until creamy smooth, stopping every now and then to scrap down the sides.

Add additional water 1 or 2 tablespoons at a time until desired consistency. If you find you added too much water, add a few more cashews and blend.

Taste for flavor, adding an extra date or two for added sweetness if desired.

Store cashew cream in an air-tight container in the fridge for up to 5 days. Sweet cream will thicken when chilled.

Makes anywhere from 1 ½ cups and up, depending on how much water you use.

TO SERVE

Place Berry Crisp in a small bowl or individual ramekin

Top with desired amount of cashew cream

Warm Release Your ImmuniTEA syrup. Drizzle with Release Your ImmuniTEA syrup on top of cashew cream

*OPTIONAL this can be served with berry crisp and Release Your ImmuniTEA only

NOTES:

*Quick soak cashews: To soak your cashews quickly, cover them with hot water and let set for 5 – 10 minutes. Drain cashews and use accordingly.

**Regular soak for cashews: Cover with an inch of cool water, let soak for 2 – 3 hours. Cashews don't need any longer than 3 hours but will be OK if soaked longer.

***You can add a little of your favorite granola to the crisp to make the flavor your own.

****You may also make individual servings in ramekins or small dishes. This recipe makes 8 servings.

Sweet & Nice & Everything Chai (Sweet Potato Chai Muffins)

INGREDIENTS

1 ¼ cup sweet potato, mashed

½ cup coconut oil, melted

½ cup maple syrup

2 eggs

2 tsp vanilla extract

1 ½ cup gluten free flour or all-purpose flour

1 ½ tsp baking soda

pinch of salt

¼ cup of pecans chopped (optional)

For the Frosting: (optional)

8 oz cream cheese, softened

2 tbsp butter, softened

1 tsp vanilla

1 cup powdered sugar

Lemon Zest (optional)

INSTRUCTIONS

Preheat the oven to 350 degrees F. Line 12 muffin tins with paper liners or spray with non-stick cooking spray and set aside.

Ground ½ tablespoon of Release Chill & Chai Tea then set aside

In a large mixing bowl, or food processor, stir/puree the mashed sweet potato until smooth.

Add the Release Chill & Chai, pecans if desired, coconut oil, maple syrup, eggs, and vanilla until smooth.

Add the flour and baking soda, and salt, mix until just combined.

Divide the batter among the prepared muffin cups. Transfer to the oven and bake for 18-20 minutes or until a toothpick inserted into the center comes out clean (Don't overbake or they will be dry!).

Store in an airtight container at room temperature. (Wait until they are completely cooled before frosting

For the Icing:

In a stand mixture or with a hand mixer, beat together the cream cheese and butter until smooth.

Add in vanilla and slowly add the powdered sugar. Add lemon zest if desired.

Beat until smooth and creamy.

Chill in the fridge for 20 minutes before frosting muffins.

Comfy-Cozy Apple Cinnamon Cookies

Comfy Cozy Tea Butter:

2 sticks of butter plus

8 Tbsp Comfy Cozy Apple Tea

INSTRUCTIONS

Melt the butter in a saucepan over low heat Add Comfy Cozy Apple tea and steep on low heat for 5 minutes. Remove from the heat and steep for 5 minutes.

Strain the leaves from the butter using a fine strainer or cheesecloth.

NOTE Some of the butter clings to the tea leaves, so use more butter than the recipe calls for when making the tea butter. Strain the tea butter into a measuring cup to make sure you have at least ¾ cup of tea butter.

Once strained, cool the butter so it solidifies.

Comfy Cozy Apple Cinnamon Cookies

¾ cup (6oz) tea butter, softened

¾ cup sugar

¾ cup light brown sugar, packed

1 egg, plus 1 egg yolk

2 tsp vanilla extract

2 ¼ cups all-purpose flour

½ tsp baking soda

½ tsp salt

1 cup Apples, peeled and chopped small (choose a firm baking apple like granny smith)

INSTRUCTIONS

Pre-heat oven to 350 and lightly grease a cookie sheet.

In an electric mixer beat the tea butter and sugars together.

Add the eggs and vanilla extract and mix until creamy.

Stir the flour, salt and soda together. Gradually add to the sugar/butter mixture until incorporated.

Fold in the apples.

Roll the dough into 1 ¼" balls (a rounded teaspoon size) and place on the greased cookie sheet.

Bake for 10-13 minutes until golden brown.

Cool on the sheet slightly before moving to a wire rack.

Enjoy with your favorite cup of tea!

I'm just a little girl from Indianapolis, "Naptown" as it is known, who had visions of other places and other worlds. That my parents never traveled to. My paternal grandmother was a traveler. She went to almost all 50 states and a few countries on 5 other continents. Though she was from a generation that did not offer a lot of opportunities and adventures to African American women, her faith and education opened doors that her great-grandparents could only pray for on the plantation in Kentucky. I got the travel bug from her. The summer that I turned nine years old, she took me on a road trip. We took about 5 days to drive from Indianapolis to New Orleans where she was attending a church missionary conference. My grandmother was a life member as was her mother in the Women's Missionary Society of the AME Church. Whenever and wherever, there was a meeting, my grandmother was there because she held many voting positions in the society. Plus, she was dedicated to service. This was the first time I ever visited New Orleans, but it wasn't my last. If you have ever been to New Orleans, you know that it is a very intoxicating city. The food, culture, the music; shoot people just move differently in New Orleans than anywhere else I have been. At nine years old, it planted something in me that drew me back for a summer program my sophomore year in high, then again as a college student. And YES! I am a PROUD alum of an HBCU. Xavier University of Louisiana to be exact. The only Black private Catholic institution of higher learning in America that sits in the Mississippi valley in the crescent bend. I returned to New Orleans in 2010 to do some volunteer work needed from hurricane Katrina, my plan was to be there two and a half weeks. I don't know what happened, but in that time with NO plan, I bought a house! That intoxicating city got me, and I was drunk! I lived there for 11 years of my life. No matter where I go, or what I do, New Orleans is always a part of me. It grew me into some for real for real "big girl panties". This chapter is dedicated to New Orleans. It was because of my experiences in New Orleans that FREEALITEA WAS created. It was in New Orleans that FREEALITEA was created. Yes, she is born and raised in New Orleans. As we say in New Orleans when you get a little something extra, here is some "lagniappe" for you. A little something extra; some extra magic you can make in your kitchen. Per Oxford's dictionary, lagniappe is something given as a bonus or extra.

Enjoy some extra recipes that use some of the herbs found in FREEALITEAs.

Creole Jambalaya with a **FREEALITEA** Spin

INGREDIENTS

3 tablespoons cooking oil, divided

2 tablespoons Slap Ya Mama/Cajun seasoning, (adjust to suit your tastes/heat preference) or Tony Chachere's

10 ounces andouille sausage, sliced into rounds

1-pound boneless skinless chicken thighs, cut into 1-inch pieces

1 onion diced

1 small green bell pepper seeded and diced

1 small red bell pepper seeded and diced

2 stalks celery, chopped

4 cloves garlic, minced

1 cup Baby Lima Beans (frozen)

14 ounces can crushed tomatoes

1 teaspoon salt

½ tsp. ground black pepper

1 tsp. each dried thyme and dried oregano

¼ tsp. Cayenne Pepper

½ tsp. hot pepper sauce

2 tsps. Worcestershire sauce

1 cup thinly sliced okra (or 1 teaspoon file powder)

1 ½ cups uncooked white rice long grain)

2 ½ cups chicken broth or vegetable stock

½ cup of Release & Relieve Turmeric tea brewed

1-pound raw shrimp tails on or off, peeled and deveined

Sliced green onions and chopped parsley, to garnish

INSTRUCTIONS

Heat 1 tablespoon of oil in a large pot or Dutch oven over medium heat. Season the sausage and chicken pieces with half of the Cajun seasoning.

Brown sausage in the hot oil; remove with slotted spoon and set aside. Add remaining oil to the pot and sauté chicken until lightly browned. Remove with slotted spoon; set aside.

Sauté the onion, bell pepper and celery until onion is soft and transparent.

Stir in the tomatoes and lima beans. Season with salt, pepper, thyme, oregano, Cayenne pepper, hot sauce, Worcestershire sauce, and the remaining Cajun seasoning. Stir in the okra slices (or file powder), chicken and sausage. Cook for 5 minutes, while stirring occasionally.

Add in the rice, garlic, Release & Relieve tea, and chicken broth, bring to a boil, then reduce heat to low-medium. Cover and let simmer for about 20 to 25 minutes, or until liquid is absorbed and rice is cooked, while stirring occasionally.

Place the shrimp on top of the Jambalaya mixture, stir through gently and cover with lid. Allow to simmer while stirring occasionally, until the shrimp are cooked through and pink (about 5-6 minutes, depending on the size/thickness of the shrimp being used).

Add extra seasonings if needed for taste and remove from heat

Top with chopped green onions and parsley

ENJOY!

NOTES

*To make Release & Relieve Turmeric tea, bring ½ cup of water to a boil. Add ½ tablespoon of Release & Relieve tea and allow to steep. Remove tea bag or loose tea after 10 minutes. Set aside

**You can make this a little healthier by removing the chicken and sausage and adding more vegetables such as zucchini, carrots, and okra.

When I attended Xavier University of Louisiana, I was introduced to gumbo, specifically seafood gumbo or chicken and sausage gumbo. If you have ever had an opportunity to have REAL gumbo, that is some that has been prepared at someone's house, then you know the ingredients can vary. I absolutely LOVED it! By the time I returned to New Orleans to live as an adult, I was a vegetarian. As much as I wanted to partake during the holidays, the pork ingredient stopped me. There were a few times I couldn't resist. The aroma coming from the pot, the look of ecstasy on people's faces as they ate, I couldn't refrain. It tasted like bliss in a bowl, but then my body would react in an unfavorable way. The I discovered Gumbo Z'herbes. A friend of mine told me about the tradition that Leah Chase was known for during the Lent season. It is a gumbo made with 9 greens! My home was in the 6th ward of New

Orleans, not far from the famous Dooky Chase restaurant. I even walked there a few times. Baby let me tell you, when I tasted it, it was EVERYTHING! I had to learn how to make this on my own so I wouldn't have to wait just once a year. The following is my version with a little **FREEALITEA** for extra umph!

FREEALITEA's Gumbo Z'herbes

INGREDIENTS

Nine Greens Such as

1 bunch Mustard greens

1 bunch Collard greens

1 bunch Turnip greens

1 bunch of Kale

1 bunch Beet tops

1 bunch Swiss Chard

1 bunch Spinach

½ head of Romaine Lettuce

½ head of Cabbage

2 cups of Release & Purify Green Tea brewed

2 medium sweet onions, chopped

6-8 Garlic, Cloves smashed

5 tbsp. all-purpose flour

2 tbsp. chopped fresh parsley

½ teaspoon cayenne pepper

1 tsp. Filé powder

1 tsp. Thyme leaves

1 tsp. Cayenne Pepper

1 tbsp. Sea Salt

Black Pepper

1 pound of spicy sausage

1 bouillon cube

Hot cooked rice, to serve

INSTRUCTIONS

Wash all the greens thoroughly removing all dirt and grit.

Rough chop them into pieces. In a large Dutch oven place greens, 2 cups of brewed Release & Purify Green tea, with garlic, onions, sea salt, pepper, and bouillon cube. Add water to the pot, enough to cover the greens. Bring mixture to a boil, reduce to simmer, cover and cook for 30 minutes.

Strain greens and set aside in a bowl. Reserve liquid.

Cut spicy sausage into bite size pieces and place in same Dutch oven with a little oil. Cook on high heat until cooked through without burning. Remove sausage, keeping the grease in the Dutch oven and set aside.

Blend greens in a food processor until pureed. Purée in batches, if needed

Heat the Dutch oven of spicy sausage grease over a high heat and whisk in flour; whisking occasionally, until roux is light golden brown, about 5 minutes.

Whisk in about 10 cups of reserve liquid. Stir to combine until smooth.

Add pureed greens to pot.

Let simmer over a low heat for 20 minutes. Add spicy sausage, thyme and cayenne, stir well. Season and simmer for 40 minutes. Stir in file powder and remove from heat.

Serve over rice. Garnish with parsley and hot sauce.

Season to taste i.e., if need to add more salt, cayenne pepper etc.

Citrus Dressing Marinade

INGREDIENTS

1 cup fresh squeezed Orange Juice

1 Lime or Lemon (fresh squeezed)

1-2 Tbsp. Fresh Parsley (chopped)

1-2 Tbsp. Fresh Chopped Basil Leaf

1 tsp. Bragg's Liquid Amino

1-2 Garlic Cloves

1oz. or more of Olive Oil

INSTRUCTIONS

Mix together

Season to Taste (Sea Salt, Pepper, Vegesal, Tony Chachere's, Herbs de Provence etc.)

This marinade is delicious with raw jicama which can be cut into strips or use as a regular salad dressing.

Apple Cider Reduction Vinaigrette

INGREDIENTS

2 cups of Apple Cider

¼ - ½ Tbsp. Apple Cider Vinegar (to taste)

Olive Oil (to desired consistency)

Fresh Squeezed Lime or Lemon Juice (to desired consistency)

Fresh Herbs (Parsley, Basil, Cilantro, Rosemary etc. depending on taste)

Bragg's Liquid Aminos

INSTRUCTIONS

Boil apple cider down until it becomes a syrup consistency (will yield approximately ¼ cup. If need more double the amount of apple cider used).

Whisk in olive oil, apple cider vinegar, Bragg's and seasoning.

Season to taste

Store unused portion in a glass jar up to 4 days.

Release Recharge Simple Syrup

INGREDIENTS

¾ cup raw honey

1 cup of brewed Release Recharge Tea

INSTRUCTIONS

Boil 1 ¼ cup of water. Once has reached a boil, turn off and add 1 tablespoon of Release Recharge tea.

Allow tea to steep for 15-20 minutes. Strain and set aside. (This can be made ahead of time)

Combine honey and Release Recharge tea in a small saucepan and warm over medium-low heat, stirring until honey dissolves completely. There is no need to bring it to a simmer.

Remove from heat and let the honey syrup cool completely.

Pour into a mason jar or other airtight glass container and store in the refrigerator.

*Can make more by doubling the recipe. Keep the 1:1 ratio

Release Your ImmuniTEA Simple Syrup

INGREDIENTS

¾ cup raw honey

1 cup of brewed Release Your ImmuniTEA Tea

INSTRUCTIONS

Boil 1 ¼ cup of water. Once has reached a boil, turn off and add 1 tablespoon of Release Your ImmuniTEA tea.

Allow tea to steep for 15-20 minutes. Strain and set aside. (This can be made ahead of time)

Combine honey and Release Your ImmuniTEA in a small saucepan and warm over medium-low heat, stirring until honey dissolves completely. There is no need to bring it to a simmer.

Remove from heat and let the honey syrup cool completely.

Pour into a mason jar or other airtight glass container and store in the refrigerator.

Release Recharge Cherry Vinaigrette

INGREDIENTS

½ cup Dried Cherries

1 cup Release Recharge Syrup

½ Pomegranate Juice

Extra Virgin Olive Oil

1 tsp. Organic Apple Cider Vinegar

INSTRUCTIONS

Heat pomegranate juice and dried cherries in a saucepan for 10 minutes. Remove cherries and set to the side.

Add Release Recharge syrup

Stir until is incorporated and pomegranate juice has thickened.

Remove while still warm and mix with olive oil, apple cider vinegar

Let cool and add to favorite dishes

CONCLUSION

By preparing some of these recipes, you have just leveled up your tea game! Who knew? This is just the tip of the iceberg. Allow this experience to open your mind and imagination to all of the innovative ways you can use teas. Tea can be used to warm us when it is cold and soothe us when we are sad. You deserve to be happy and healthy! You deserve a stress-FREE reality and allowing yourself to experience pleasure every day. Teas, especially combined with certain herbs can help take you there. Stay tuned because as my Godfather used to always say, "You ain't seen nothing yet!"

May these recipes help you create magical meals and me-time moments.

THANK YOU

I would like to thank my great grandparents Frank Black and Edna Burnett Black for their love and wisdom. Frank Black, the father of Nanny, was the seventh son, born in the seventh month in 1873. He practiced the wisdom of ancient healing practices through the mastery of herbs. Many of the herbs he used to help people were grown in the garden that my grandparents created and named, The Victory Garden. Before helping someone, he would ask, "Do you believe that you can be healed?" Depending on their answer, he would proceed. Whatever the doctor's couldn't cure with their medication; Frank Black had something for it! He said that the special knowledge could only be given to a relative born in the seventh month. I stand today and honor this knowledge and tradition as Dr. Michelle born in the seventh month, on the seventh day in 1971.

May my ancestors be proud and continue to guide and cheer me on!

Be well!

Dr. Michelle

Website: www.freealitea.com

Facebook: www.facebook.com/freealitea.co

Instagram: www.instagram.com/freealitea.co/

NOTES

NOTES

www.ingramcontent.com/pod-product-compliance
Lightning Source LLC
Chambersburg PA
CBHW061756290426
44109CB00030B/2874